The Underground Railroad:
Life on the Road to Freedom

edited by Ellen Hansen

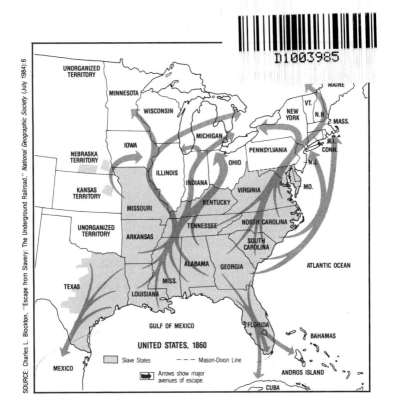

© Discovery Enterprises, Ltd.
Lowell, Massachusetts
1993

© Discovery Enterprises, Ltd., Lowell, MA 1993

ISBN 1-878668-27-7 paperback edition
Library of Congress Catalog Card Number 93-72239

10   9   8   7   6   5   4   3   2   1

Printed in the United States of America

Subject Reference Guide:
Underground Railroad
Abolition of Slavery
David Walker – *The Appeal*
Harriet Tubman
William Lloyd Garrison – *The Liberator*

Credits
The "Caution" poster and the reading on David Walker are reprinted courtesy of the Museum of Afro American History, Boston Massachusetts.

Cover illustration from *The Anti-Slavery Record*, Vol. III, No. VII (July, 1837).

Source for illustration of major Underground Railroad routes: Charles L. Blockson, "Escape from Slavery: The Underground Railroad," *National Geographic* magazine (July 1984).

Photographs and illustrations on pages 8, 20, 30, and the cover are reprinted with the permission of the Boston Athenaeum, Boston, Massachusetts.

Acknowledgments
For all their help, I thank the staffs of the Boston Athenaeum, the Boston Public Library, the Mugar Memorial Library (Boston University), the Museum of Afro American History (Boston), and the National Park Service (both the Boston staff at the African Meeting House and the Colorado staff doing the Underground Railroad study).

Table of Contents

Dedication

*For my parents, Jim and Louise, whose
courage in constructing their own lives and beliefs
has shown me the way.*

Foreword

The Underground Railroad was neither "underground" nor a "railroad." It was a network of people and houses throughout sixteen northern U.S. states and Canada, organized to help escaped slaves reach safety.

At that time (about 1820 - 1860), such activities were against the law. Underground Railroad workers and fugitive slaves therefore had to carry on in secret - often in darkness or disguise. As many as 100,000 fugitive slaves traveled the Underground Railroad's "lines" (or routes) north to freedom.

Slaves, mainly people of African descent, had been seeking freedom from bondage since colonial times. Even as white colonists sought their own human rights and independence from Britain during the latter 1700's, blacks were forced to sue for their freedom in court or take great risks in running away from their masters. The invention of the cotton gin and the passage of the first national fugitive slave law (both in 1793) seemed to give new life to this "peculiar institution" of slavery, which was so tied into the economy of the South.

By the early 1800's, fugitive slaves had many sympathizers in the North, including free blacks, abolitionists, and church groups such as the Quakers, Congregationalists, and Methodists. These "agents" of the Underground Railroad ran "safe houses" to harbor the escaping slaves on their way north; served as "conductors" leading the fugitives to the next "station" or resting place; raised money, collected food and clothing for the cause; and worked politically (starting newspapers, giving speeches, working to get laws passed) to end slavery.

The courage and perseverance of the fugitive slaves, combined with these efforts by the "agents," formed the backbone of the Underground Railroad.

This book explores the most active years of the Underground Railroad - the three or four decades leading up to the Civil War. There are many names worthy of mention in any discussion of the Underground Railroad and the anti-slavery movement: Harriet Tubman, Frederick Douglass, Abraham Lincoln, William Lloyd Garrison, Levi Coffin, Robert Purvis, William Still, Lucretia Mott, Anthony Burns, Susan B. Anthony, Ellen and William Craft, David Walker, Elijah Lovejoy, Sarah and Angelina Grimke, Thomas Garrett, Harriet Beecher Stowe, James Brown, and Nat Turner, for example. One selection in this book, James Adams's story of his escape, is included as a tribute to the countless others involved in the Underground Railroad whose names are lost to history.

You'll find both primary and secondary sources here. Primary sources are oral histories, songs, newspaper articles, letters, speeches, and other records from the period being studied. The articles, essays, and textbooks which historians later write, based on those primary sources, are secondary sources.

The first reading is the daring tale of how Ellen and William Craft made their way north to freedom.

William and Ellen Craft
as reported in William Still's book
The Underground Rail Road (1871): 382 - 384.

*Female Slave in Male Attire, Fleeing As a Planter,
with Her Husband As Her Body Servant*

A quarter of a century ago, William and Ellen
Craft were slaves in the State of Georgia. With them,
as with thousands of others, the desire to be free was
very strong. For this jewel they were willing to make
any sacrifice, or to endure any amount of suffering. In
this state of mind they commenced planning. After
thinking of various ways that might be tried, it occurred to William and Ellen, that one might act the
part of master and the other the part of servant.

Ellen being fair enough to pass for white, of necessity would have to be transformed into a young
planter for the time being. All that was needed, however, to make this important change was that she
should be dressed elegantly in a fashionable suit of
male attire, and have her hair cut in the style usually
worn by young planters. Her profusion of dark hair
offered a fine opportunity for the change. So far this
plan looked very tempting. But it occurred to them
that Ellen was beardless. After some mature reflection, they came to the conclusion that this difficulty
could be very readily obviated by having the face

Ellen and William Craft

muffled up as though the young planter was suffering badly with the face or toothache; thus they got rid of this trouble. Straightway, upon further reflection, several other very serious difficulties stared them in the face. For instance, in traveling, they knew that they would be under the necessity of stopping repeatedly at hotels, and that the custom of registering would have to be conformed to, unless some very good excuse could be given for not doing so.

Here they again thought much over matters, and wisely concluded that the young man had better assume the attitude of a gentleman very much indisposed. He must have his right arm placed carefully in a sling; that would be a sufficient excuse for not registering, etc. Then he must be a little lame, with a nice cane in the left hand; he must have large green spectacles over his eyes, and withal he must be very hard

8

of hearing and dependent on his faithful servant (as was no uncommon thing with slave-holders), to look after all his wants.

William was just the man to act this part. To begin with, he was very "likely-looking;" smart, active and exceedingly attentive to his young master -- indeed he was almost eyes, ears, hands and feet for him. William knew that this would please the slave-holders. The young planter would have nothing to do but hold himself subject to his ailments and put on a bold air of superiority; he was not to deign to notice anybody. If, while traveling, gentlemen, either politely or rudely, should venture to scrape acquaintance with the young planter, in his deafness he was to remain mute; the servant was to explain. In every instance when this occurred, as it actually did, the servant was fully equal to the emergency -- none dreamed of the disguises in which the Underground Rail Road passengers were traveling.

They stopped at a first-class hotel in Charleston, where the young planter and his body servant were treated, as the house was wont to treat the chivalry. They stopped also at a similar hotel in Richmond, and with like results.

They knew that they must pass through Baltimore, but they did not know the obstacles that they would have to surmount in the Monumental City. They proceeded to the depot in the usual manner, and the servant asked for tickets for his master and self. Of course the master could have a ticket, but "bonds will have to be entered before you can get a ticket," said

the ticket master. "It is the rule of this office to re-
quire bonds for all negroes applying for tickets to go
North, and none but gentlemen of well-known re-
sponsibility will be taken," further explained the ticket
master.

The servant replied, that he knew "nothing about
that" -- that he was "simply traveling with his young
master to take care of him -- he being in a very deli-
cate state of health, so much so, that fears were enter-
tained that he might not be able to hold out to reach
Philadelphia, where he was hastening for medical
treatment," and ended his reply by saying, "my master
can't be detained." Without further parley, the ticket
master very obligingly waived the old "rule," and furnished the requisite tickets. The mountain being thus
removed, the young planter and his faithful servant
were safely in the cars for the city of Brotherly Love.

Scarcely had they arrived on free soil when the
rheumatism departed -- the right arm was unslung --
the toothache was gone -- the beardless face was un-
muffled -- the deaf heard and spoke -- the blind saw --
and the lame leaped as an hart, and in the presence of
a few astonished friends of the slave, the facts of this
unparalleled Underground Rail Road feat were fully
established by the most unquestionable evidence.

David Walker's *Appeal*

Not all blacks during this time were slaves. Some, like David Walker, were born free blacks; others purchased their own freedom or had their freedom purchased for them by friends, family members, or religious groups.

David Walker believed that blacks should fight for their freedom by any means possible, including violent means. In this respect, he went further than most abolitionists at the time.

The following selection about David Walker is reprinted in its entirety from The African Meeting House* in Boston - A Sourcebook.**

David Walker was a free black man, born in Wilmington, North Carolina on September 28, 1785. After travelling extensively in the South and observing first-hand the effects of slavery, he came to Boston in 1827. Here he opened a shop on Brattle Street where he sold both new and second-hand clothing. White clothing dealers tried to force him out of business, and Walker and two other black clothing dealers were subjected to police harassment. In 1828, they were indicted and tried for receiving stolen goods.

*See notes, p. 57.
**Reprinted *courtesy of the Museum of Afro American History.*

Walker and one of the others were acquitted, and charges against the third were dropped.

Walker quickly became involved in the black community, working to improve education for black children, establish black churches, and increase employment opportunities for blacks. He became a leader in the Massachusetts General Colored Association, an organization founded in 1826 to abolish slavery and improve racial conditions for blacks. He was Boston's agent for and occasional contributor to *Freedom's Journal*, or *Rights of All*, as it was renamed by Samuel Cornish in 1829, after Russwurm resigned and went to Liberia.

Walker is remembered, however, for a pamphlet that he published in 1829. Known as *Walker's Appeal*, the full title of the seventy-six page pamphlet was *Walker's Appeal, in Four Articles: Together with a Preamble, to the Coloured Citizens of the World, but in particular, and very expressly, to those in the United States of America, written in Boston, State of Massachusetts, September 28, 1829.* The four articles mentioned in the title address four separate issues: Article 1 deals with slavery and its evil consequences; Article 2, with the black's lack of education; Article 3 addresses the upholding of the slave system by the Christian ministry; and Article 4 is concerned with the colonization plan.* Much of Walker's appeal is addressed particularly to slaves, urging them to rise up and take the freedom due them, by any means possible.

*See notes, p. 57.

Never make an attempt to gain our freedom or natural right, from under our cruel oppressors and murderers, until you see your way clear -- when that hour arrives and you move, be not afraid or dismayed ...

... if you commence ... kill or be killed. Now, I ask you, had you not rather be killed than to be a slave to a tyrant, who takes the life of your mother, wife and dear little children? ... believe this, that it is no more harm for you to kill a man, who is trying to kill you, than it is for you to take a drink of water when thirsty ...

Walker also addressed part of his message to white Americans:

If any are anxious to ascertain who I am, know the world, that I am one of the oppressed, degraded and wretched sons of Africa, rendered so by the avaricious and unmerciful, among the whites. If any wish to plunge me into the wretched incapacity of a slave, or murder me for the truth, know ye, that I am in the hand of God, and at your disposal. I count my life not dear unto me, but I am ready to be offered at any moment. For what is the use of living, when in fact I am dead. But remember, Americans, that as miserable, wretched, degraded and abject as you have made us in preceding, and in this generation, to support you and your families, that some of you (whites) on the continent of America, will yet curse the day that you ever were born. You want slaves, and want us for your slaves!!! My colour will yet, root some of you out of the very face of the earth!!!!!!

The Appeal was the most militant and inflammatory anti-slavery document that had ever been published, and response to it was immediate and intense. The South was enraged; a reward was offered for Walker -- $1,000 dead or $10,000 alive. Georgia and South Carolina passed laws against incendiary publications -- Georgia made the circulation of such documents a capital offense. The governor of Georgia and the mayor of Savannah sent letters to Boston's mayor urging him to suppress the publication. The mayor replied that he didn't like the pamphlet either, but that no law had been broken and there was nothing he could do.

Four blacks were arrested in New Orleans for distributing the "diabolical Boston pamphlet." The vigilance committee of South Carolina offered a $1500 reward for the arrest of anyone distributing *The Appeal*. The document came under attack even among northerners and abolitionists; Benjamin Lundy claimed it would injure the cause, Samuel May attributed to it a rise in southern fury against the Abolitionists; Garrison, however, referred to it as "one of the most remarkable productions of the age" and the "forerunner of the Abolition struggle."

Reaction against Walker was so strong that he was urged to go to Canada, but he insisted on remaining in Boston, in spite of, or perhaps because of, the furor aroused by *The Appeal.* It was in its third printing in 1830, when Walker's body, possibly dead of poisoning, was found outside his shop. Although he had been in Boston only three years, Walker left his mark on the city and on the anti-slavery movement. He also left a son, Edward Garrison Walker, who became a lawyer prior to the Civil War, and in 1866 was elected to the Massachusetts House of Representatives, representing Charlestown. He and Charles L. Mitchell, elected at the same time, were the first blacks to sit on any state legislature.

Sometimes looking at the whole gives a deeper meaning to the parts. The next section is a chronology of the anti-slavery movement, from the arrival of the first African laborers to America's shores in 1619 to the Thirteenth Amendment's abolition of slavery in 1865. The chronology is excerpted and adapted from the Museum of Afro American History's Sourcebook *and the National Park Service's publication* Taking the Train to Freedom.

Chronology

1619	The first African laborers are shipped to Virginia.
1641	Massachusetts colony legalizes slavery.
1642	Virginia colony passes law to fine anyone harboring or assisting runaway slaves.
1660	Virginia colony legalizes slavery.
1775	The first Quaker anti-slavery society, the Society for the Relief of Free Negroes Unlawfully Held in Bondage, is organized in Philadelphia.
1776	North American colonies declare independence from Great Britain.
1777-1804	Northern states abolish slavery through state constitutions and gradual abolition laws.
1787	The Northwest Ordinance bans slavery in the Northwest Territory.
1793	Fugitive Slave Act becomes a federal law, providing for the return of slaves escaped across state boundaries.
1794	The first national anti-slavery society, The American Convention for Promoting the Abolition of Slavery, is founded.
1807	Congress passes a law prohibiting the importation of slaves into the U.S. after January 1, 1808.
1818	As a response to the Fugitive Slave Act of 1793, abolitionists use the "underground" to assist slaves to escape into Ohio and Canada.
1820	The Missouri Compromise admits Missouri as a slave state; Maine as a free state; and establishes

the 36° 30' parallel of latitude as the dividing line between free and slave areas of the territories.

1821   Benjamin Lundy, a Quaker, starts publishing his anti-slavery paper, the *Genius of Universal Emancipation.*

1822   Former slave Denmark Vesey leads a slave uprising in Charleston, South Carolina.

1829   Black abolitionist David Walker issues *David Walker's Appeal.* Afterwards, several slave revolts occurred throughout the South.

1830   Levi Coffin leaves North Carolina, settles in Indiana and continues abolitionist activities.

1831   William Lloyd Garrison prints first issues of his anti-slavery newspaper, *The Liberator.*

1831-   Virginia constitutional convention narrowly defeats
1832   emancipation. The Nat Turner Rebellion takes place in Virginia.

1832   Louisiana presents resolution requesting federal government to arrange with Mexico to permit runaway slaves from Louisiana to be reclaimed when found on foreign soil.

In Boston, Garrison founds the New England Anti-Slavery Society, urging immediate emancipation.

1833   Slavery ends in the British Empire.

The American Anti-Slavery Society is founded in Philadelphia.

1834   The moderate and church-oriented American Union for the Relief and Improvement of the Colored Race is founded by Massachusetts Congregational ministers.

1837   Elijah Lovejoy's press is destroyed, and Lovejoy is killed in Alton, Illinois.

1838	Underground Railroad is "formally organized." Black abolitionist Robert Purvis becomes chairman of the General Vigilance Committee and "president" of the Underground Railroad.
1839	*American Slavery As It Is: Testimony of a Thousand Witnesses*, edited by Sarah and Angelina Grimke and Theodore D. Weld, is published. It exposes atrocities and outrageous conditions under slavery.
1840	The World Anti-Slavery Convention is held in London. Women are denied seats on the floor.
1842	Supreme Court rules in *Prigg v. Pennsylvania* that state officials are not required to assist in the return of fugitive slaves.
1845	Frederick Douglass prints *Narrative of the Life of Frederick Douglass*, an account of his slave experience and escape to freedom.
1847	Douglass begins publishing his anti-slavery newspaper, the *North Star.*
1849	Harriet Tubman makes her escape from Maryland.
1850	Compromise of 1850 attempts to settle slavery issue. As part of the Compromise, a new Fugitive Slave Act is added to enforce the 1793 law and allows slaveholders to retrieve slaves in northern states and free territories.
1852	Harriet Beecher Stowe's *Uncle Tom's Cabin* is published. It broadens and popularizes the anti-slavery debate.
1854	The Kansas-Nebraska Bill is passed, stirring up civil war in Kansas Territory over the slavery issue. The fugitive slave Anthony Burns is returned from Boston to Virginia. Over 2,000 federal troops are called out to ensure his return.

1857 In the *Dred Scott* case, the Supreme Court declares that blacks are not U.S. citizens, and that slaveholders have the right to take slaves in free areas of the country.

1858 Abraham Lincoln condemns slavery in his "House Divided" speech.

1859 John Brown's failed raid on federal arsenal and armory in Harper's Ferry, which was aimed at starting a general slave insurrection.

1860 Republican candidate Abraham Lincoln is elected President of the United States.

1861 Civil War begins.

1863 President Lincoln issues the Emancipation Proclamation which declares "all persons held as slaves within any state...be in rebellion against the United States shall be then...forever free."

1865 Civil War ends.
      The Thirteenth Amendment to the U.S. Constitution is ratified, abolishing slavery permanently.

Hopping "On Board" the Underground Railroad

One of the more memorable escapes from slavery was that of Henry "Box" Brown. He hit upon the idea of being crated up, and shipped direct to Philadelphia as freight. Brown stepped into the box a slave in Richmond, Virginia, and emerged twenty-six hours later in Philadelphia a free man.

The box measured three feet long, two feet wide, and two feet eight inches deep, and was lined with baize. Brown's only supplies were one small container of water, a few biscuits, and a handtool to bore holes for air. A friend nailed the box up and strapped

Resurrection of Henry Box Brown.

20

the outside with five hickory hoops, marking the box "This side up with care" near the address.

Nonetheless, Brown spent a good deal of time on his head during the journey, as the box was transferred from dray to train to ferry to wagon. When the box arrived at its destination, the Anti-Slavery Society offices in Philadelphia, one of those expecting him rapped quietly on the box, calling out "All right?" "All right, sir!" came the answer from within. When the hoops were cut and the lid lifted, Brown stood up in the box, reached out his hand and said, "How do you do, gentlemen?"

Such a spectacular escape, though, was the exception. Most runaway slaves did just that - *run away*. They relied on their own courage, instinct, and stamina to escape the inhumane life of a slave.

The news passed quickly from plantation to plantation among the slaves: "There's an Underground Railroad that leads north -- to freedom." But how did they make the initial escape from their plantations? Where did the slaves learn the routes to follow? Once on their way, how did they evade the slave hunters and bloodhounds pursuing them, and where did their arduous journey end?

Few were as bold as Ellen and William Craft, traveling in disguise by day and on major routes. Most runaway slaves traveled at night using the North Star as their guide, and made their escape alone or in small groups. Usually, they left on Saturday night. This gave them a head start: their absence wouldn't be noticed until Monday when they were summoned back into the fields to work.

Before reaching the free states and the nearest "safe house" on the Underground Railroad, the fugitives hid by day in barns, in haystacks, in the woods. At night, they'd press on, avoiding the well-traveled routes and sticking to backroads, fields, forests, swamps, and waterways.

Some slaves had learned the song "Follow the Drinking Gourd" (meaning the Big Dipper) and so knew how to locate the North Star using that constellation. Others had seen anti-slavery pictures on handkerchiefs smuggled in with goods arriving from the North, or seen the "scatter sheets" (anti-slavery pamphlets) left by Underground Railroad workers along roadsides and other places accessible to slaves.

Word about the "underground" spread. Slaves "hired out" by their masters to work temporarily at other plantations spread the word. Friends and relatives visiting on a Sunday from a nearby plantation spread the word. And Underground Railroad workers whose jobs involved travel through the South, such as handymen, mechanics, preachers and salesmen, spread the word. These northern workers occasionally provided slaves with money toward their escape as well.

Word-of-mouth communication about the Underground Railroad worked best for two reasons: most slaves couldn't read, and those who could were not allowed to read anti-slavery material. The information which passed from person to person gave details about how to "ride the rails."

Slaves learned how to recognize a safe house in the North: a quilt (with a house and smoking chimney as one of its designs) hanging on a clothesline; a lamp (of a certain brightness) in the window; a ring of white bricks around a house's chimney.

They also learned of possible water routes to freedom, for instance getting "hired out" aboard a steamboat on the Ohio River or stowing away on coastal shipping vessels headed for seaports in the North. Anti-slavery crews in northern ports then helped fugitives make the escape at that end.

Reaching a safe house in the North meant food, clothing, and added protection against capture. But it did not yet mean freedom, especially in states bordering the South.

When the Fugitive Slave Act passed in 1850, runaway slaves weren't safe until they arrived in Canada, which was beyond the reach of the slave hunters. Therefore, "traveling the rails" meant staying hidden, even once they were "on board" the Underground Railroad.

Slaves were hidden in the attics, storerooms, and cellars of safe houses; in secret chambers and behind false walls; under mattresses of feather beds. While in transit to the next stopping place, Underground Railroad "conductors" hid slaves under bales of goods in wagons, as stowaways aboard ships, and in the woods. They were all risking capture. Capture meant a return to slavery for the runaways, and a fine of $1,000 and six months in jail for underground agents.

The Fugitive Slave Act of 1850 prompted the more well-known escaped slaves such as Ellen and William Craft, Frederick Douglass, and William Wells Brown, to flee to Europe to avoid capture. That Act also spelled danger for free blacks in the North: free blacks and escaped slaves alike were being captured by slave hunters and brought down South to be sold into slavery. Many free blacks fled to Canada to avoid that risk.

The issue of slavery was tearing the nation apart. Abraham Lincoln, while campaigning for a senate seat in 1858, put it this way: "A house divided against itself cannot stand. I believe this government cannot endure, permanently half *slave* and half *free*."

The Civil War (1861-1865) began three years later. On September 22, 1862, President Lincoln issued the Emancipation Proclamation, which declared that as of January 1, 1863, "all persons held as slaves within any state ... in rebellion against the United States shall be then ... and forever free."

The Civil War had been ennobled: it was now being fought to save the union *and* to abolish slavery. In 1865, the Civil War ended and the Thirteenth Amendment to the U.S. Constitution was ratified, abolishing slavery permanently.

The Underground Railroad, which had grandly served its purpose, was no longer needed.

A North-Side View of Slavery
The Refugee: or the Narratives of Fugitive Slaves in Canada, by Benjamin Drew (Boston, 1855)

In 1855, Boston educator and journalist Benjamin Drew went to Canada to collect narratives from among the estimated 30,000 fugitive slaves there. That same year, he published their stories, which described the horrors of slavery and the runaways' escape from that "peculiar institution," as A North-Side View of Slavery.

Drew's book was in direct response to three occurrences of the previous year: (1) passage of the Kansas-Nebraska Bill of 1854, which left the existence of slavery in each new territory up to the voters in such territory; (2) the capture and conviction (under the Fugitive Slave Law of 1850) of runaway slave Anthony Burns in Boston, and the 2,000 federal troops called out to ensure Burns's return to slavery amid abolitionist protest; and (3) the publication of A South-Side View of Slavery *by Reverend Nehemiah Adams of Boston, which suggested that slaveowners be regarded as "the guardians, educators, and saviors of the African race in this country."*

This selection from A North-Side View of Slavery *is the narrative of James Adams, a resident of St. Catharines, Ontario.*

JAMES ADAMS

I was raised in Virginia, about twenty miles above the mouth of the Big Kanawha. At the age of seventeen, I set out to seek freedom in company with Benjamin Harris, (who was a cousin of mine)... I was young, and they had not treated me very badly; but I had seen older men treated worse than a horse or a hog ought to be treated; so, seeing what I was coming to, I wished to get away. My father being overseer, I was not used so badly as some even younger than myself, who were kicked, cuffed, and whipped very badly for little or nothing. We started away at night, on the 12th of August 1824. After we had crossed the river, alarm was given, and my father came down where we had crossed, and called to me to come back. I had not told my intention to either my father or mother. I made no answer at all, but we walked three miles back from the river, where we lay concealed in the woods four days. The nights we passed at the house of a white friend; a friend indeed. We set out on a Monday night, and on the night following, seven more of my fellow-servants started on the same race. They were overtaken on Wednesday night, while they were in a house on the Ohio side. One jumped from a window and broke his arm; he stayed in the woods some days, and then he returned. The other six, two women and four children, were carried back, and the man we stopped with told us that the two women were whipped to make them tell where we were, so they could come upon us. They told their master as near as they could. On Thursday five white men came to the house where we had been concealed, but we were then in the woods and mountains, three miles from the friend's house. Every evening, between three and four o'clock, he would come and bring us food. We had nothing to give him -- it was the hand of Divine Providence made him do it. He and others on the river see so much abuse of colored people that they pity them, and so are ready to give them aid; at least it was so then. He told the white men he knew nothing about us, and nothing of the kind. They searched his premises, and then left, believing his story. He came to us and said, "Boys, we are betrayed, they are coming now round the hill after us." We picked up our bundles and started on a run; then he called us back, and said he did it to try our *spunk*. He then told us of those who were carried back, and of the searching of his premises. We lodged in his barn that night ...

[Later in our escape, a friend] pointed out a haystack, where we were to rendezvous at night, to meet another man whom our friend was to send to take us further along on our way. At night we went to the haystack; a road ran by it. Instead of keeping watch by the stack, we were so jaded that we crossed the road and lay down to rest on the bare ground, where we fell asleep. The man, as we afterwards learned from him, came as agreed upon, whistled and made signals, but failed to wake us up. Thinking we had been pursued away, he went back without us. The next morning, when we awoke, the sun was rising red, right on the public road. We saw a man at his door some two hundred yards from us. I went to ask him how the roads ran; [Ben] told me to inquire the way to Carr's Run, near home, so we would go the contrary. By the time I got back, Ben, who had watched, saw the man leave his house with his gun, and take a circle round to come down on us; but before he could head us, we were past him in the road running. We ran and walked about four miles barefoot; then we took courage to put on our shoes, which we had not dared stop long enough to do before, for fear the man with the gun would get ahead of us. ...

Presently we came to a toll-gate, about which there were standing several white men. We walked up boldly to the gate; one of the men then asked us, "Where are you going?" Ben answered, "We are going to Chillicothe to see our friends there." Then he made answer and said, "You can't go any further, you must go back with me, you are the very boys I was looking for last night." We told him we wanted to go on, but he said, "There are so many buckskin Yankees in these parts that you will be taken before you get half through the town." We then went back to his house, but we did not stop more than ten minutes, because it would be dangerous for him as well as for us if we were caught on his premises. He stuck up a pole close to his house and tied a white cloth on it; then he led us up to the top of the hill (this was Monday, quite early in the morning), and showed us a rough place of bushes and rocks where we could lie concealed quite pleasantly, and so high up that we could see the main road, and the toll-gate, and the house, and the white flag. Said he, "If there's any danger, I'll send a child out to throw down the white flag; and if you get scared away from here, come back at night and I'll protect you." Soon after he left us, we saw five white men come to his house on horseback; they were the five who had carried back the others that tried to escape. Two of them went into the house; then we saw a little girl come out and climb up on the fence, as if she were playing about, and she knocked down the flag-pole -- which meant that we were to look out for ourselves. But we did not feel that there was any immediate danger, and so we kept close under cover. Pretty soon the two came out of the house, and they all rode forward very fast, passed the toll-gate, and were soon out of sight. I suppose they thought to overtake us every minute, but luckily I have never seen them since. In the evening the man came and conducted us to his house, where we found the men we had seen at the toll-gate in the morning. They were mostly armed with pistols and guns. They guided us to a solitary house three miles back among the mountains, in the neighborhood of which we remained three days. We were told to go up on the mountain very high, where was an Indian cave in the rocks. From this cave we could look a great distance around and see people, and we felt afraid they would see us. So instead of staying there, we went down the mountain to a creek where trees had been cut down and branches thrown over the bank; we went under the branches and bushes where the sand was dry, and there we would sit all day. We all the time talked to

THE

ANTI-SLAVERY RECORD.

Vol. III. No. VII.   JULY, 1837.   Whole No. 31.

This picture of a poor fugitive is from one of the stereotype cuts manufactured in this city for the southern market, and used on handbills offering rewards for runaway slaves.

each other about how we would get away, and what we should do if the white folks tackled us; that was all our discourse.

We stayed there until Friday, when our friends gave us knapsacks full of cakes and dried venison, and a little bundle of provision besides, and flints and steel, and spunk, and a pocket-compass to travel through the woods by. We knew the north-star, but did not travel nights for nearly a week. So on Friday morning we set out, the men all bidding us good-by, and the man of the flag-staff went with us half a day to teach us the use of the compass; we had never seen one before. Once in a while he would put it on a log to show us how to travel by it. When he was leaving us, he took his knife and marked on the compass, so that we should steer a little west of north.

During the six days succeeding, we traversed an unbroken wilderness of hills and mountains, seeing neither man nor habitation. At night we made a fire to sit by. We saw deer on our way; we were not annoyed by wild animals, and saw but one snake, a garter-snake. The first sign of man we met with was a newly-made road; this was on the seventh day from the time we left the house in the mountains. Our provisions held out well, and we had found water enough. After crossing the road, we came out from the mountains to a level cleared place of farms and houses. Then we were afraid, and put ourselves on our guard, resolving to travel by night. We laid by until starlight, then we made for a road leading to the north. We would follow a road until it bent away from the north; then we would leave it and go by the compass. This caused us to meet many rivers and streams where there were no bridges; some we could wade over, and some we crossed by swimming. After reaching the clearings, we scarcely dared build a fire. Once or twice we took some green corn from the fields, and made a brush fire to roast it. After lighting the fire, we would retire from it, as far almost as we could see it, and then watch whether anybody might come to it. When the fire had gone out, the corn would be about done.

Our feet were now sore with long travelling. One night we came to a river; it was rather foggy, but I could see a ferry-scow on the other side. I was afraid of alligators, but I swam over, and poled the scow back and ferried Ben across, - his ankle was so sore, that he did not like to put his foot in the water if he could help it. We soon reached an old stable in the edge of a little town; we entered it and slept alternately one keeping watch, as we always managed while in the neighborhood of settlements. We did not do this in the wilderness, -- *there* we slept safely, and were quite *reconciled*. At cock-crowing in the morning we set out and went into the woods, which were very near; there we stayed through the day.

At night we started on and presently came into a road running north-west. Coming to a vine patch we filled our knapsacks with cucumbers; we then met a white man, who asked us, "Which way are you travelling?" My cousin told him "To Cleveland, to help a man drive a drove of cattle." He then said, "I know you must be runaways, -- but you needn't be afraid of me, -- I don't want to hurt you." He then told us something that we knew before -- that the last spring five fugitives were overtaken at his house by my master and two other men; that the fugitives took through his wheat-field, -- one of them, a little fellow, could not run so fast as the rest, and master called to him to stop, or he'd shoot him. His answer was, "shoot and be d--d!" The man further told us, that he took through the wheat-field as if he would assist in catching the slaves, but that when he got near enough, he told them to "push on!" Ben and I knew about the pursuit, and what the little fellow had said; for it got round among the servants, after master got back. That little fellow's widow is now my wife. We went to the man's house, and partook of a good luncheon. He told us to hurry, and try to get through Newark [Ohio] before daylight. We hurried accordingly, but it was daybreak when we crossed the bridge. We found the little toll-gate open and we went through -- there were lights in a tavern window at the left of the gate, and the windows had no curtains. Just as we were stepping off the bridge, a plank rattled, -- then up started after us a little black dog, making a great noise. We walked smartly along, but did not run until we came to a street leading to the right, -- then we ran fast until we came to a left hand turn, which led to the main road at the other side of the town. Before sunrise, we hid in a thicket of briars, close by the road, where we lay all day, seeing the teams, and every thing that passed by.

At dark we went on again, passed through Mount Vernon [Ohio] in the night, and kept on until daylight. Again we halted in concealment until night, then we went on again through Wooster. After leaving Wooster, we saw no more settlements, except one little village, which we passed through in broad day. We entered a store here, but were asked no questions. Here we learned the way to Cleveland. In the middle of the afternoon we stopped for a little rest. Just before night we moved forward again and travelled all night. We then stopped to rest until four in the afternoon, meanwhile roasting some corn as before. At about four, we met a preacher, who was just come from Cleveland. He asked us if we were making our escape, -- we told him "No." He said, "You need not be afraid of me, -- I am the friend of all who travel from the South to the North." He told us not to go into Cleveland, as we would be taken up. He then described a house which was on our way, where, he said, we might mention our meeting him, and we would find friends who would put us on board a boat. We hid until dark, -- then we went to the house, which we recognized readily from the preacher's description. We knocked at the door, and were invited in. My cousin told them what the minister had said. The man of the house hid us in his barn two nights and three days. He was a shoemaker. The next night after we got there, he went to Cleveland himself to get a berth for us aboard some boat for Canada. When he returned, he said he had found a passage for us with Capt. B., who was to sail the next Thursday at 10,

P.M. At that hour we embarked, having a free passage in a schooner for Buffalo. On board this boat, we met with an Englishman whom we had often seen on a steamboat at the plantation. He knew us, and told us a reward of one hundred dollars was offered for each of us, and he showed us several handbills to that effect. He said they had been given him to put up along the road, but he had preferred to keep them in his pocket. Capt. B. took away our knives and Ben's tomahawk, for fear of mischief.

We reached Buffalo at 4, P.M. The captain said, that if there was any danger in the town, he would take us in his yawl and put us across. He walked through the town to see if there were any bills up. Finding no danger, he took us out of the hatchway, -- he walked with us as far as Black Rock Ferry, giving us good advice all the way, how we should conduct ourselves through life in Canada, and we have never departed from his directions, -- his counsel was good, and I have kept it.

I am now buying this place. My family are with me, -- we live well, and enjoy ourselves. I worship in the Methodist church. What religious instruction I received on plantation, was from my mother.

I look upon slavery as the most disgusting system a man can live under. ... Men who have never seen or felt slavery cannot realize it for the thing it is. If those who say that fugitives had better go back, were to go to the South and *see* slavery, they would never wish any slave to go back.

I have seen separations by sales, of husbands from wives, of parents from children, -- if a man threatens to run away, he is sure to be sold. Ben's mother was sold down South -- to New Orleans -- when he was about twenty years old.

I arrived in Canada on the 13th September, 1824.

Note: The narratives, newspaper articles, and other readings in this book have been reprinted as they were originally written. For this reason, you may notice some archaic spellings and expressions, as well as inconsistent spelling and capitalization from reading to reading.

Moses

from *The Freedmen's Record*,
Vol. 1, No. 3 (Boston, March, 1865): 34-38.

Perhaps the most famous "conductor" on the Underground Railroad was Harriet Tubman. After escaping from slavery herself in 1849, she returned to the South again and again, at great risk, to lead others to freedom. Thus, she earned the title Moses. *The following article about Harriet Tubman was published by the New-England Freedmen's Aid Society in their monthly publication* The Freedmen's Record.

One of the teachers lately commissioned by the New-England Freedmen's Aid Society is probably the most remarkable woman of this age. That is to say, she has performed more wonderful deeds by the native power of her own spirit against adverse circumstances than any other. She is well known to many by the various names which her eventful life has given her; Harriet Garrison, Gen. Tubman, &c.; but among the slaves she is universally known by her well-earned title of *Moses*, -- Moses the deliverer. She is a rare instance, in the midst of high civilization and intellectual culture, of a being of great native powers, working powerfully, and to beneficient ends, entirely unaided by schools or books.

Her maiden name was Araminta Ross. She is the granddaughter of a native African, and has not a drop of white blood in her veins. She was born in 1820 or 1821, on the Eastern Shore of Maryland. Her parents were slaves, but married and faithful to each other, and the family affection is very strong. She claims that she was legally freed by a will of her first master, but his wishes were not carried into effect.

She seldom lived with her owner, but was usually "hired out" to different persons. She once "hired her time," and employed it in rudest farming labors, ploughing, carting, driving the oxen, &c., to so good advantage that she was able in one year to buy a pair of steers worth forty dollars.

When quite young she lived with a very pious mistress; but the slaveholder's religion did not prevent her from whipping the young girl for every slight or fancied fault. Araminta found that this was usually a morning exercise; so she prepared for it by putting on all the thick clothes she could procure to protect her skin. She made sufficient outcry, however, to convince her mistress that her blows had full effect; and in the afternoon she would take off her wrappings, and dress as well as she could. ...

In her youth she received a severe blow on her head from a heavy weight thrown by her master at another slave, but which accidentally hit her. The blow produced a disease of the brain which was severe for a long time, and still makes her very lethargic. She cannot remain quiet fifteen minutes without appearing to fall asleep. It is not refreshing slumber;

but a heavy, weary condition which exhausts her. She therefore loves great physical activity, and direct heat of the sun, which keeps her blood actively circulating. She was married about 1844 to a free colored man named John Tubman, but never had any children. Owing to changes in her owner's family, it was determined to sell her and some other slaves; but her health was so much injured, that a purchaser was not easily found. At length she became convinced that she would soon be carried away, and she decided to escape. Her brothers did not agree with her plans; and she walked off alone, following the guidance of the brooks, which she had observed to run North. The evening before she left, she wished very much to bid her companions farewell, but was afraid of being betrayed, if any one knew of her intentions; so she passed through the street singing, --

"Good bye, I'm going to leave you,

Good bye, I'll meet you in the kingdom," --
and similar snatches of Methodist songs. ...

[After escaping across the Mason-Dixon Line into a free state,] she remained two years in Philadelphia working hard and carefully hoarding her money. Then she hired a room, furnished it as well as she could, bought a nice suit of men's clothes, and went back to Maryland for her husband. But the faithless man had taken to himself another wife. Harriet did not dare venture into her presence, but sent word to her husband where she was. He declined joining her. At first her grief and anger were excessive. ... [B]ut finally she thought ... "if he could do without her, she could without him," and so "he dropped out of her heart," and she determined to give her life to brave deeds. Thus all personal aims died out of her heart; and with her simple brave motto, "I can't die but once," she began the work which has made her Moses, -- the deliverer of her people. Seven or eight times* she has returned to the neighborhood of her former home, always at the risk of death in the most terrible forms, and each time has brought away a company of fugitive slaves, and led them safely to the free States, or to Canada. Every time she went, the dangers increased. In 1857 she brought away her old parents, and, as they were too feeble to walk, she was obliged to hire a wagon, which added greatly to the perils of the journey. In 1860 she went for the last time, and among her troop was an infant whom they were obliged to keep stupefied with laudanum to pre-vent its outcries. This was at the period of great ex-citement, and Moses was not safe even in New-York State; but her anxious friends insisted upon her taking refuge in Canada. So various and interesting are the incidents of the journeys, that we know not how to select from them. She has shown in them all the characteristics of a great leader: courage, foresight, prudence, self-control, ingenuity, subtle perception, command over others' minds. ...

A clergyman once said, that her stories convinced you of their truth by their simplicity as do the gospel narratives. She never went to the South to bring away fugitives without being provided with money; money

*See notes, p. 57.

for the most part earned by drudgery in the kitchen, until within the last few years, when friends have aided her. She had to leave her sister's two orphan children in slavery the last time, for the want of thirty dollars. Thirty pieces of silver; an embroidered hand-kerchief or a silk dress to one, or the price of freedom to two orphan children to another! She would never allow more to join her than she could properly care for, though she often gave others directions by which they succeeded in escaping. She always came in the winter when the nights are long and dark, and people who have homes stay in them. She was never seen on the plantation herself; but appointed a rendezvous for her company eight or ten miles distant, so that if they were discovered at the first start she was not com-promised. She started on Saturday night; the slaves at that time being allowed to go away from home to visit their friends, -- so that they would not be missed until Monday morning. Even then they were supposed to have loitered on the way, and it would often be late on Monday afternoon before the flight would be certainly known. If by any further delay the advertisement was not sent out before Tuesday morning, she felt secure of keeping ahead of it; but if it were, it required all her ingenuity to escape. She resorted to various de-vices, she had confidential friends all along the road. She would hire a man to follow the one who put up the notices, and take them down as soon as his back was turned. She crossed creeks on railroad bridges by night, she hid her company in the woods while she herself not being advertised went into the towns in search of information. If met on the road, her face was always to the south, and she was always a very respectable looking darkey, not at all a poor fugitive. She would get into the cars near her pursuers and manage to hear their plans. ...

The expedition was governed by the strictest rules. If any man gave out, he must be shot. "Would you really do that?" she was asked. "Yes," she replied, "if he was weak enough to give out, he'd be weak enough to betray us all, and all who had helped us; and do you think I'd let so many die just for one coward man." "Did you ever have to shoot any one?" she was asked. "One time," she said, a man gave out the second night; his feet were sore and swollen, he couldn't go any further; he'd rather go back and die, if he must." They tried all arguments in vain, bathed his feet, tried to strengthen him, but it was of no use, he would go back. Then she said, "I told the boys to get their guns ready, and shoot him. They'd have done it in a minute; but when he heard that, he jumped right up and went on as well as any body." She can tell the time by the stars, and find her way by natural signs as well as any hunter; and yet she scarcely knows of the existence of England or any other foreign country.

When going on these journeys she often lay alone in the forests all night. Her whole soul was filled with awe of the mysterious Unseen Presence, which thrilled her with such depths of emotion, that all other care and fear vanished. Then she seemed to speak with her Maker "as a man talketh with his friend;" her child-like petitions had direct answers, and beautiful visions lifted her up above all doubt and anxiety into serene trust and faith. No man can be a hero without this faith in some form; the sense that he walks not in his own strength, but leaning on an almighty arm. Call it fate, destiny, what you will, Moses of old, Moses of to-day, believed it to be Almighty God. ...

Her efforts were not confined to the escape of slaves. She conducted them to Canada, watched over their welfare, collected clothing, organized them into societies, and was always occupied with plans for their benefit. ...

She has a very affectionate nature, and forms the strongest personal attachments. She has great simplicity of character; she states her wants very freely, and believes you are ready to help her; but if you have nothing to give, or have given to another, she is content. She is not sensitive to indignities to her color in her own person; but knows and claims her rights. She will eat at your table if she sees you really desire it; but she goes as willingly to the kitchen. She is very abstemious in her diet, fruit being the only luxury she cares for. Her personal appearance is very peculiar. She is thoroughly negro, and very plain. She has needed disguise so often, that she seems to have command over her face, and can banish all expression from her features, and look so stupid that nobody would suspect her of knowing enough to be dangerous; but her eye flashes with intelligence and power when she is roused. ...

The Fugitive Slave Act of 1850

The first federal law governing the return of slaves who had escaped across state boundaries was passed in 1793. The Fugitive Slave Act of 1850 amended and enlarged the scope of that law. Portions of the 1850 Act are excerpted below.

Fugitive Slave Act
Thirty-first Congress
Sess. I Ch. 60 (1850)

Be it enacted by the Senate and House of Representatives of the United States of America in congress assembled,

...That when a person held to service or labor in any State or Territory of the United States, has heretofore or shall hereafter escape into another State or Territory of the United States, the person or persons to whom such service or labor may be due, or his, her, or their agent or attorney, ... may pursue and reclaim such fugitive person, either by procuring a warrant ... or by seizing and arresting such fugitive, where the same can be done without process, and by taking, or causing such person to be taken, forthwith before such court, judge, or commissioner, whose duty it shall be to hear and determine the case of such claimant in a summary manner; and upon satisfactory proof being made, by deposition or affidavit, ... or by other satisfactory testimony, duly taken and certified ... to make out and deliver to such claimant, his or her agent or attorney, a certificate setting forth the substantial facts as to the service or labor due from such fugitive to the claimant, and of his or her escape from the State or Territory in which such service or labor was due, to the State or Territory in which he or she was arrested, with authority to such claimant, or his or her agent or attorney, to use such reasonable force and restraint as may be necessary, under the circumstances of the case, to take and remove such fugitive person back to the State or Territory whence he or she may have escaped as aforesaid. *In no trial or hearing under this act shall the testimony of such alleged fugitive be admitted in evidence*; [emphasis added] and the certificates ... shall be conclusive of the right of the person or persons in whose favor granted, to remove such fugitive to the State or Territory from which he escaped, and shall prevent all molestation of such person or persons by any process issued by any court, judge, magistrate, or other person whomsoever.

And be it further enacted, That any person who shall knowingly and willingly obstruct, hinder, or prevent such claimant, his agent or attorney, or any person or persons lawfully assisting him, her, or them, from arresting such a fugitive from service or labor, either with or without process as aforesaid, or shall rescue, or attempt to rescue, such fugitive from service or labor, from the custody of such claimant, his or her agent or attorney, or other person or persons lawfully assisting as aforesaid, when so arrested, pursuant to the authority herein given and declared; or shall aid, abet, or assist such person so owing service or labor as aforesaid, directly or indirectly, to escape from such claimant, his agent or attorney, or other person or persons legally authorized as aforesaid; or shall harbor or conceal such fugitive, so as to prevent the discovery and arrest of such person, after notice or knowledge of the fact that such person was a fugitive from service or labor as aforesaid, shall, for either of said offences, be subject to a fine not exceeding one thousand dollars, and imprisonment not exceeding six months, by indictment and conviction before the District Court of the United States for the district in which such offence may have been committed, or before the proper court of criminal jurisdiction, if committed within any one of the organized Territories of the United States; and shall moreover forfeit and pay, by way of civil damages to the party injured by such illegal conduct, the sum of one thousand dollars, for each fugitive so lost as aforesaid, to be recovered by action of debt, in any of the District or Territorial Courts aforesaid, within whose jurisdiction the said offence may have been committed. ...

APPROVED, September 18, 1850.

CAUTION!!

COLORED PEOPLE

OF BOSTON, ONE & ALL,

You are hereby respectfully CAUTIONED and advised, to avoid conversing with the

Watchmen and Police Officers of Boston,

For since the recent ORDER OF THE MAYOR & ALDERMEN, they are empowered to act as

KIDNAPPERS

AND

Slave Catchers,

And they have already been actually employed in KIDNAPPING, CATCHING, AND KEEPING SLAVES. Therefore, if you value your LIBERTY, and the *Welfare of the Fugitives* among you, *Shun* them in every possible manner, as so many *HOUNDS* on the track of the most unfortunate of your race.

Keep a Sharp Look Out for KIDNAPPERS, and have TOP EYE open.

APRIL 24, 1851.

The Fugitive Slave Act of 1850 further specified that: there would be no trial by jury in fugitive cases; a federal marshal could be fined $1,000 for refusing to arrest a fugitive slave, and if any fugitive escaped while in his care (whether the marshal's fault or not), the marshal was liable for the value of the slave; and the fee for the commissioner deciding a fugitive case would be ten dollars if he found for the master, five dollars if he freed the slave.

William Lloyd Garrison

William Lloyd Garrison was an outspoken white abolitionist. His newspaper The Liberator *spanned the most active years of the Underground Railroad, from the 1830's through the passage of the Thirteenth Amendment in 1865. Garrison initially argued for gradual abolition, but soon became committed to immediate and unconditional emancipation. What follows is an excerpt from his "Manifesto," which appeared in the first issue of* The Liberator *(Jan. 1, 1831).*

The Liberator

In defending the great cause of human rights, I wish to derive the assistance of all religions and of all parties.

Assenting to the "self-evident truth" maintained in the American Declaration of Independence, "that all men are created equal, and endowed by their creator with certain inalienable rights - among which are life, liberty and the pursuit of happiness," I shall strenuously contend for the immediate enfranchisement of our slave population. ...

I am aware, that many object to the severity of my language; but is there not cause for severity? I *will be* as harsh as truth, and as uncompromising as justice. On this subject, I do not wish to think, or speak, or write, with moderation. No! no! Tell a man whose house is on fire, to give a moderate alarm; tell him to moderately rescue his wife from the hands of the ravisher; tell the mother to gradually extricate her babe from the fire into which it has fallen; -- but urge me not to use moderation in a cause like the present. I am in earnest -- I will not equivocate -- I will not excuse -- I will not retreat a single inch -- AND I WILL BE HEARD.

William Lloyd Garrison
Boston, January 1, 1831

On December 18, 1865, the Thirteenth Amendment to the Constitution was ratified, permanently abolishing slavery. The full Amendment was published in Garrison's abolitionist newspaper four days later.

The Liberator
Boston, Friday, December 22, 1865

OFFICIAL PROCLAMATION
DECLARING
"Liberty throughout all the land, unto
all the inhabitants thereof."

WILLIAM H. SEWARD, SECRETARY OF STATE
OF THE UNITED STATES, TO ALL TO WHOM THESE
PRESENTS MAY COME, GREETING:

Know ye, that whereas the Congress of the United
States, on the 1st of February last, passed a Resolution, which is in the words following, viz.:

"A Resolution submitting to the Legislatures of the
several States a proposition to amend the Constitution
of the United States:

Resolved, by the Senate and the House of Representatives of the United States of America, in Congress assembled, two-thirds of both Houses concur-
ring, that the following article be proposed to the
Legislatures of the several States as an amendment to
the Constitution of the United States, which, when
ratified by three-fourths of said Legislatures, shall be
valid to all intents and purposes as part of said Constitution, viz.:

ARTICLE XIII. SECTION 1. NEITHER SLAVERY NOR
INVOLUNTARY SERVITUDE, EXCEPT AS A PUN-
ISHMENT FOR CRIME, WHEREOF THE PARTY
SHALL HAVE BEEN DULY CONVICTED, SHALL
EXIST WITHIN THE UNITED STATES, OR ANY
PLACE SUBJECT TO THEIR JURISDICTION.

SECTION 2. Congress shall have power to enforce this
article by appropriate legislation."

And whereas, it appears from official documents
on file in this Department, that the amendment to the
Constitution of the United States, proposed as aforesaid, HAS BEEN RATIFIED by the Legislatures of the
States of Illinois, Rhode Island, Michigan, Maryland,

New York, West Virginia, Ohio, Missouri, Nevada, Indiana, Louisiana, Minnesota, Wisconsin, Vermont, Tennessee, Arkansas, Connecticut, New Hampshire, Maine, Kansas, Massachusetts, Pennsylvania, Virginia, South Carolina, Alabama, North Carolina -- in all, twenty-seven [sic] States;

And whereas, the whole number of States in the United States is thirty-six;

And whereas, the before specially named States, whose Legislatures have ratified the said proposed amendment, constitute three-fourths of the whole number of States in the United States:

Now, therefore, be it known that I, William H. Seward, Secretary of the United States, by virtue and in pursuance of the second section of the act of Congress, approved on the 20th day of April, 1818, entitled "An act to provide for the publication of the laws of the United States, and for other purposes, do hereby certify that THE AMENDMENT AFORESAID HAS BECOME VALID, TO ALL INTENTS AND PURPOSES, AS PART OF THE CONSTITUTION OF THE UNITED STATES.

In testimony whereof I have hereunto set my hand, and caused the seal of the Department of State to be affixed.

Done at Washington, this 18th day of December, in the year of our Lord 1865, and of the Independence of the United States of America the ninetieth.

WILLIAM H. SEWARD,
Secretary of State.

Spirituals

Spirituals are religious folk songs which grew out of the sufferings of black Americans in slavery. They were sung long before the Proclamation of Emancipation, or the Thirteenth Amendment's permanent abolition of slavery. No one knows their exact origin, for they were carried by slaves from plantation to plantation, from state to state.

Frederick Douglass knew the miseries of slavery firsthand, and later described the meaning of spirituals this way:

> They breathed the prayer and complaint of souls boiling over with the bitterest anguish. Every tone was a testimony against slavery, and a prayer to God for deliverance from chains. The hearing of those wild notes always depressed my spirit, and filled me with ineffable sadness. ... These songs still follow me, to deepen my hatred of slavery, and quicken my sympathies for my brethren in bonds. ... The songs of the slave represent the sorrows of his heart; and he is relieved by them, only as an aching heart is relieved by its tears.

Here are the words to two spirituals: Nobody Knows De Trouble I See *and* Swing Low, Sweet Chariot.

Nobody Knows De Trouble I See

Chorus
Nobody knows de trouble I see,
   Nobody knows but Jesus;
Nobody knows de trouble I see,
   Glory hallelujah!

Sometimes I'm up, sometimes I'm down,
   Oh, yes, Lord;
Sometimes I'm almost to de groun',
   Oh, yes, Lord.

Altho' you see me goin' 'long so,
   Oh, yes, Lord;
I have my trials here below,
   Oh, yes, Lord.

Chorus
Oh, nobody knows de trouble I see,
   Nobody knows but Jesus;
Nobody knows de trouble I see,
   Glory hallelujah!

Swing Low, Sweet Chariot

Chorus
Swing low, sweet chariot,
  Comin' for to carry me home,
Swing low, sweet chariot,
  Comin' for to carry me home.

I look'd over Jordan an' what did I see,
  Comin' for to carry me home,
A band of angels comin' after me,
  Comin' for to carry me home.

If you get there before I do,
  Comin' for to carry me home,
Tell all my friends I'm comin' there too,
  Comin' for to carry me home.

Chorus
Swing low, sweet chariot,
  Comin' for to carry me home,
Swing low, sweet chariot,
  Comin' for to carry me home.

Definitions

abolition - legal termination of slavery in the United States

Anti-Slavery Society - an organization dedicated to the abolition of slavery (sometimes called *Abolition Society* or *Freedmen's Aid Society*)

baize - a cotton or woolen material napped to imitate felt

dray - a low, heavy cart without sides, for hauling things

emancipate - to free from oppression or bondage; liberate

fugitive - a person who flees; a runaway

laudanum - a tincture of opium, used to quiet crying babies while en route on the Underground Railroad

Mason-Dixon line - the border between Maryland and Pennsylvania, regarded as the boundary of "the South"

Quakers - members of the religion called the Society of Friends. The term was first used by church leaders, who told members to "tremble at the word of the Lord."

safe house - Underground Railroad term for houses of people involved in helping slaves escape

scow - a large flat-bottomed boat with square ends, used chiefly for transporting freight

spunk - tinder (used to start fires); also, spirit, resourceful courage in the face of difficulties

Notes

African Meeting House, Boston (p. 11): the oldest black church built by free blacks still standing in America. Since 1806, it has served as a church, a school, a gathering spot for abolitionists, and a place for celebrations and political meetings. William Lloyd Garrison founded the New England Anti-Slavery Society, which was committed to "immediate and unconditional emancipation," in this building on January 6, 1832.

Colonization plan (p. 12): The American Colonization Society, founded in 1816, proposed combining a gradual abolition of slavery with the resettlement of emancipated slaves in West Africa. "Tell us no more about colonization," declared Walker in his *Appeal*, "for America is as much our country as it is yours." By the 1830's, the colonization approach had fallen into disfavor. The abolitionist movement now demanded immediate emancipation, based on the moral conviction that slavery was an outright evil and that it contradicted the core values embodied in the Declaration of Independence.

Seven or eight times (p. 40): Accounts differ as to how many trips Harriet Tubman made to the South. Some historians believe she made nineteen trips, leading more than 300 slaves out of bondage.

Bibliography

Abrahams, Roger D. *Singing the Master*. New York: Pantheon Books, 1992.

Aptheker, Herbert, ed. *A Documentary History of the Negro People in the United States*. New York: The Citadel Press, 1951.

Blassingame, John W., ed. *Slave Testimony - Two Centuries of Letters Speeches, Interviews, and Autobiographies*. Baton Rouge: Louisiana State University Press, 1977.

Blockson, Charles. *The Underground Railroad -- First-Person Narratives of Escapes to Freedom in the North*. New York: Prentice Hall Press, 1987.

Chapman, Abraham, ed. *Steal Away*. New York: Praeger Publishers, 1971.

Douglass, Frederick. *Life and Times of Frederick Douglass - Written By Himself*. New York: The MacMillan Co., 1962 (reprint of his fourth and final autobiography, originally published in 1892).

Drew, Margaret A. and Parsons, William S. *The African Meeting House in Boston - A Sourcebook*. Boston, The Museum of Afro American History, 1990.

Five Black Lives. Middleton, Conn.: Wesleyan University Press, 1971 (narratives first published between 1798 and 1881).

Four Fugitive Slave Narratives. Reading, Mass: Addison-Wesley Publishing Co., 1969 (narratives first published between 1847 and 1881).

Jefferson, Paul, ed. *The Travels of William Wells Brown* New York: Markus Wiener Publishing, Inc., 1991 (first published in 1847).

Pennington, James W.C. *The Fugitive Blacksmith*. Westport, Conn.: Negro Universities Press, 1971 (first published in 1850).

Quarles, Benjamin. *Black Abolitionists*. New York: Oxford University Press, 1969.

Siebert, Wilbur H. *The Underground Railroad: From Slavery to Freedom*. New York: The MacMillan Co., 1898.

Stampp, Kenneth M. *The Peculiar Institution - Slavery in the Ante-Bellum South*. New York: Alfred A. Knopf, 1956.

Still, William. *The Underground Rail Road - A Record of Facts, Authentic Narratives, Letters*. Chicago: Johnson Publishing Company Inc., 1970 (first published in 1871).

Further Reading for Students

Chittenden, Elizabeth F. *Profiles in Black and White - Stories of Men and Women Who Fought Against Slavery.* New York: Charles Scribner's Sons, 1973.

Cosner, Shaaron. *The Underground Railroad.* New York: Franklin Watts, 1991.

Freedman, Florence B. *Two Tickets to Freedom - The True Story of Ellen and William Craft, Fugitive Slaves.* New York: Peter Bedrick Books, 1971.

Hamilton, Virginia. *Anthony Burns: The Defeat and Triumph of a Fugitive Slave.* New York: Alfred A. Knopf, 1988.

Khan, Lurey. *One Day, Levin ... He Be Free - William Still and the Underground Railroad.* New York: E.P. Dutton & Co., Inc., 1972.

Petry, Ann. *Harriet Tubman - Conductor on the Underground Railroad.* New York: Simon & Schuster, 1955.

Russell, Sharman Apt. *Frederick Douglass - Abolitionist Editor.* New York: Chelsea House Publishers, 1988.

Scott, John Anthony. *Hard Trials on My Way: Slavery and the Struggle Against It, 1800-1860.* New York: Alfred A. Knopf, Inc., 1974.

Taylor, M.W. *Harriet Tubman - Antislavery Activist.* New York: Chelsea House Publishers, 1991.

About the Author

Ellen Hansen is currently a freelance writer, and writes for the Boston Sunday Globe, the Boston Business Journal, and the Christian Science Monitor. She is also the author of *The New England Transcendentalists* in this Perspectives on History Series.

She has a B.A. in Languages and Political Science from Middlebury College and a J.D. from American University Law School. After practicing law for a number of years, she taught German and English in Japan for three years. She is a perpetual student, fascinated by looking at history and life through the eyes of different cultures and peoples.

Ms. Hansen lives with her husband in Boston, within blocks of the Harriet and Lewis Hayden House (an Underground safe house which sheltered Ellen and William Craft, among other fugitives); the African Meeting House; and the John J. Smith House (his barbershop was a front for Underground activities). The alley pictured above, directly behind their apartment building, is described on Boston's Black Heritage Trail as a short cut used by fugitives to get to safe houses.

Other books in the
Perspectives on History Series:

The Lowell Mill Girls: Life in the Factory
ISBN 1-878668-06-4

Voices from the West: Life Along the Trail
ISBN 1-878668-18-8

The New England Transcendentalists:
Life of the Mind and of the Spirit
ISBN 1-878668-22-6

Faith Unfurled: The Pilgrims' Quest for Freedom
ISBN 1-878668-24-2

Coming to America: A New Life in a New Land
ISBN 1-878668-23-4

Forward into Light: The Struggle for Women's Suffrage
ISBN 1-878668-25-0

Pride and Promise: The Harlem Renaissance
ISBN 1-878668-30-7

The Cherokee Nation: Life Before the Tears
ISBN 1-878668-26-9

Each book in this series is $4.95.

Fill out the order form on the reverse side and mail to Discovery Enterprises, Ltd. 134 Middle St., Suite 210, Lowell, MA 01852 or call 800-729-1720 to charge on (MC/VISA) M-F 8AM-5PM. You may also fax your orders 24 hours daily to 508-937-5779 (please include purchase order number.)

Order Form

Ship to:
Name: _____

Address: _____

City: _____ State: _____ Zip: _____

Phone: _____ P.O. Number (if applicable): _____

ISBN (last 3 digits)	Title	Qty	Total
		Sub Total	
		Shipping/Handling	
		Total	

Please add $1.50 per book shipping/handling or $5.00 for any orders over $19.00.